HELLO, GRANDMA?

by Bil Keane

FAWCETT GOLD MEDAL • NEW YORK

A Fawcett Gold Medal Book

Published by Ballantine Books

ISBN 0-449-14169-1

This edition published by arrangement with
The Register & Tribune Syndicate, Inc.

Manufactured in the United States of America

First Fawcett Gold Medal Edition: September 1973
First Ballantine Books Edition: December 1983
Second Printing: June 1984

"That's my Grandma. She used to be my daddy's
mother when he was little."

"Stop using up all the light, Billy!"

"Wake up, Daddy! It's startin' to snow, and
you said the next time it snowed you'd
help us build a snow man!"

"Here are your glasses,
Grandma!"

"The worst part about this real cold weather is
we don't get any recess."

"We started sex education today. They taught us which was the little girls' room and which was the little boys' room."

"I'm jotting down all the cute things the
children say and do. So far I've only
had time to fill half a page."

"Gee, Mommy, sometimes you're real nice --
just like a sitter!"

"A quarter? John Lincicome's tooth fairy left
FIFTY CENTS!"

"Do I have to have a reason?"

"It's a FERMASTAT and it heats the whole house."

"They didn't let me finish smiling."

"I can't eat with this hand -- I petted Barfy
with it."

"It's my time to relax -- PJ is taking a nap."

"Billy's class is having a surprise birthday party
for their teacher, but it's still
two months away."

"That's not your eyebrow pencil, Mommy. It's the pencil from my connect the dots set."

"You didn't draw ANYTHING, PJ! This is
nothing but scribble-scrabble."

"Can you help me with this composition, Mommy? It's called 'Why I Love the Winter'?"

"Why do I have to wash my hands? The dirt
won't show on a BROWNIE!"

"Why don't you use your TELEPHONE
voice, Mommy?"

"Miss Johnson is wearing a new dress and new
shoes. She wasn't sick yesterday --
she was shopping."

"I forgot to tell you, Mommy --you're s'posed
to make me a pirate costume for the
school play tomorrow."

"Close that door, Barfy! We're not tryin' to
heat the whole neighborhood, y'know."

"...For all these things we thank you, God."

"God said, 'You're welcome.'"

"Can I flush the toaster?"

"The bus didn't come, so I said you'd drive us to school."

"Stop that laughin', Dolly, 'cause Mommy said they'll SHRINK when she washes them!"

"I can't get out 'cause I forgot to wear
some shoes."

"I think Mommy's kidding us -- she says we're buying Grandma some TOILET WATER!"

"Mommy! Grandma's more than ONE year old, isn't she?"

"Grandma didn't get anything to PLAY with."

"I was just testin' your knee-flexes."

"You're right, Mommy. He's into something!"

"You're not allowed to sit in the living room,
and you can't use the bathroom towels or eat
the cake! We're havin' company tonight!"

"No, Grandma! We never get this kind of
bacon, and Mommy doesn't buy THOSE
paper towels! That's not OUR
kind of peanut butter..."

"I got the mail for you, Mommy!"

"Is this done enough to eat?"

"I've been cryin' since you went to answer the phone and now I can't 'member why I'm cryin'."

"We had an eye test today! I got a 20!"

"Mommy! How do you turn the new milk bottle off?"

"I couldn't eat my sandwich today -- it
stayed frozen!"

"You'll find the restrooms on the second floor
THROUGH the TOY DEPARTMENT..."

"Could I take a walk down the street? Grandma
said Christmas is just around the corner."

"You don't have to spell, Mommy, just go ahead
and talk. We're not listening."

"The Christmas stuff is up, Daddy! When are we goin' to put the lights up on OUR house?"

"How can you be talkin' to Santa? You didn't even dial."

"Can we open them NOW? Grandma didn't put
'Don't Open 'Til Christmas' stickers on them."

"Don't look, Daddy! We're buying your present!"

"Then Santa brought baby Jesus in his sleigh and laid him in a manger."

"They're for Barfy and Sam."

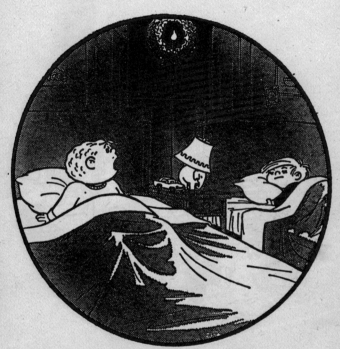

"How can we tell if visions of sugarplums are
dancing in our heads? I've never
seen a sugarplum."

"If Santa is still over at the shopping center,
maybe he'd fix this for me."

"I have to throw these bulbs away 'cause the
batteries in 'em wore out."

"I'll be right back as soon as I check on
the children."

"Are you sure this is a New Year? It looks the same as the OLD year."

"Very good, P.J! It says: 'Dear Grandma, How are you? I am fine..."

"Oh, brudder! I wanted it to say 'Dear Unca Bob'!"

"Mommy! Daddy's taking a nap on the bed with all the clean clothes! Shall I get him off?"

"I can't come out 'cause I'm sick in bed with a cold."

"You said you were having some of the GIRLS over, Mommy. They're all big LADIES!"

"Know how I can tell I'm grown up? I can reach the bathroom glass now."

"Grandma, is this fruit the kind for looking at
or the kind for eating?"

"I can't take those cookies in for our class party.
I told Miss Johnson YOU'D bake them."

"Have you seen my bug that got away, Mommy?
It's 'bout this big and it's black and has wings."

"Can't we just RIDE PAST the ice cream store on the way home?"

"Stop it, PJ, or I'll give you a good tickling."

"Mommy's birthday is in March and Daddy's is in October, so Mommy's OLDER!"

"That one's from the day I had the virus."

"ATTAWAYTOGO, MOMMY! Now you're
starting to move! Nineteen to TWO!"

"Can we go out now? God just turned off
the sky."

"Mommy! I hurt myself THIS MUCH!"

"PJ is naughty -- he wipes his mouth on his
sleeve after Aunt Nancy kisses him."

"I drew the cover on my social studies report too good. Miss Johnson says Daddy helped me."

"Mommy, how old was I when I was borned?"

"You didn't brush your teeth! I can't smell
any toothpaste!"

"The box is empty, Mommy! Can we send away
for the free plane?"

"What are we having for dessert so I know how
much room to leave?"

"Can I hold my own face while you comb my hair?"

"MOMMY! PHONE!"

"Mommy, here's something the Easter Bunny
could put in our baskets -- or does he
have enough stuff already?"

"Wish I could've talked when I was borned. I'd
have named me Patricia."

"Mommy! Jeffy won't let me offer him the sign of peace!"

"Aunt Tess and Uncle Gordon won't be here 'til dinnertime! Come in and have your lunch!"

"Hi, Aunt Tess! When are you and Uncle Gordon going home?"

"You're sleeping in OUR room...that's the
hamper for your dirty clothes...the
bathroom's right there..."

"If you and Uncle Gordon want any toys to play
with, they're in this bottom drawer."

"We forgot to tell you, Aunt Tess--there's no lock on this door."

"Lift ME up like that, Uncle Gordon?"
"Me next!"
"Me!"

"Aunt Tess, I have to get this paper signed.
Will YOU sign it?"

"Mommy! Daddy kissed Aunt Tess goodbye!
Is that okay?"

"The field trip wasn't any fun -- the principal
went, too."

"I'm home, Mommy! Nothin' to do 'til September!"

"You didn't do it right, Daddy. You were
s'posed to go flying over my shoulder!"

"We'll be there in a minute, Mommy--as soon
as we finish diggin' to China!"

"But, on the box it shows mothers and fathers playing, too."

"Come on past, Mommy! I won't squirt you!"

"If you don't eat all your food you'll grow up
into a MIDGET."

"Mommy, do we like kitty-cats?"

"Mommy! That kitty-cat got into our house!"

"Mommy, we keep saying 'go home, kitty-cat' ---
but she just keeps hanging around here!"

"I think Barfy's allergic to cats."

"I'm glad we're keeping kitty-caf, Mommy,
'cause I NEEDED a footwarmer!"

"That's okay. Cats are allowed up on things but dogs aren't."

"Listen! Her motor's running!"

"The lady on Romper Room said it's time for juice and cookies."

"Look at us, Mommy! We're helpin' Daddy!"

"Kittycat just loves our bird -- she spends all her
time guarding it."

"Ooooh! She has THORNS in her feet!"

"Can I use that towel, Mommy, or is it just
for people?"

"How do you spell 'Me'? --And don't go
too fast."

"There's a naughty fly around here. Can you
hand me the fly whipper?"

"Now, put your hand up here, Daddy...and
your foot over here..."

"Mommy! Barfy thinks you're yellin' at HIM!"

"Why don't you and Daddy go on 'The
Newlywed Game'?"

"Mommy, kittycat is trying to lie in the sunlight
but PJ keeps getting in the way."

"I planted peas, carrots, corn, squash, tomatoes,
onions, lettuce, string beans, pumpkins
and watermelons."

"I don't WANT to ride it in the parade! It looks funny!"

"Are these the people we bought the steaks for
or are they the ones for the hamburgers?"

"I'll guard the cookies for you, Mommy."

"Shh! I tell you I CAN! I can HEAR it—people talking on the telephone!"

"A fine time for the fire engines to go up the street! Right, Mommy? I guess we better go look, too."

"Clarissa knows better names for all the parts of our body than we do."

"Don't be a dummy, PJ -- you can't pull yourself
while you're in the wagon. You have
to get out to do it."

"All the dishes are in the dishwasher, so I'm
eating my ice cream out of this ash tray."